The Library of Author Biographies™

Karen Cushman

The Library of Author Biographies™

KAREN
CUSHMAN

Susanna Daniel

rosen
central™

The Rosen Publishing Group, Inc., New York

To future Catherines, Matildas, Alyces, and Rodzinas

Published in 2006 by The Rosen Publishing Group, Inc.
29 East 21st Street, New York, NY 10010

First Edition

Library of Congress Cataloging-in-Publication Data

Daniel, Susanna.
Karen Cushman / by Susanna Daniel.—1st ed.
    p. cm.—(The library of author biographies)
Includes bibliographical references (p.   ) and index.
ISBN 1-4042-0463-6 (library binding)
1. Cushman, Karen—Juvenile literature. 2. Authors, American—20th century—Biography—Juvenile literature. 3. Children's stories—Authorship—Juvenile literature. I. Title. II. Series.
PS3553.U743Z64 2005
813'.54—dc22
                                                                              2004028076

Manufactured in the United States of America

Excerpts from *Matilda Bone* by Karen Cushman. Text copyright © 2002 by Karen Cushman. Reprinted by permission of Clarion Books, an imprint of Houghton Mifflin Company. All rights reserved.

From *Something About the Author*, by Alan Hedblad, 147, Gale Group, © 2000, Gale Group. Reprinted by permission of the Gale Group.

Excerpts from *Catherine, Called Birdy* by Karen Cushman. Text copyright © 1994 by Karen Cushman. Reprinted by permission of Clarion Books, an imprint of Houghton Mifflin Company. All rights reserved.

San Francisco Chronicle index. Newspaper index by Alex Madrigal. Copyright © 1996 by *San Francisco Chronicle*. Reproduced with permission of *San Francisco Chronicle* in the Textbook format via Copyright Clearance Center.

Excerpts from *The Ballad of Lucy Whipple* by Karen Cushman. Copyright © 1996 by Karen Cushman. Reprinted by permission of Clarion Books, an imprint of Houghton Mifflin Company. All rights reserved.

"Author Spotlight: Karen Cushman" interview by Stephanie Loer from the Houghton Mifflin Education Place® web site (http://www.eduplace.com/author/cushman/interview.html). Copyright © 1999 by Houghton Mifflin Company. Reprinted by permission of Houghton Mifflin Company. All rights reserved.

Table of Contents

Introduction: Traveling Backward in Time

The female protagonists of author Karen Cushman's five young adult novels live very differently from what many modern-day people might consider to be normal. They have fleas in their beds, there is garbage on the street outside their homes, and they spend cold nights with only the heat from a dying fire. Matilda, from Cushman's fourth novel, *Matilda Bone* (2001), lives on a street named Blood and Bone Alley, where a man uses leeches (aquatic worms that suck blood) to heal the sick. Catherine, from Cushman's first novel, *Catherine, Called Birdy* (1994), which was named a Newbery Honor Book, blacks out her teeth with soot and puts mouse bones in her hair when a man she doesn't like comes over for dinner. And Brat, from *The Midwife's Apprentice* (1995), sleeps in a heap of rotting food and animal droppings in order to keep warm. (*The Midwife's Apprentice* won the Newbery Medal in 1996. The Newbery Medal is a distinguished award given annually to the most important contribution to American children's literature during the course of the prior year. Newbery Honors are given each year to just a few other titles that deserve special recognition.)

Certainly, this is all very strange. Leeches are almost never used in modern medicine. Garbage is put in cans and taken away to landfills, not used for comfort and warmth. And you might find mouse bones in a corner in a basement, but you certainly wouldn't find them where Catherine does: in the living room of her parents' home.

Matilda, Catherine, and Brat aren't aliens from a different planet; they are pretty normal for their time, which is the Middle Ages. Also called the medieval age, the Middle Ages was the period of European history from about AD 500 to about the year 1500. Catherine, for example, lives in a manor in England in the year 1290, which was long before the United States and Canada even existed as official nations, and Brat lives in England in the early 1300s. Within the world of young adult fiction, these novels are part of a genre called historical fiction. Novels that place imaginary characters in the realm of historically accurate settings, such as the Middle Ages, World War II, or even a more recent time such as the civil rights era, are all examples of historical fiction.

Why would a writer want to go to all the extra trouble of writing a book that is set in another era? Isn't writing a novel difficult enough? Sure it is, but according to Cushman, there's something particularly special about historical fiction, especially historical fiction for young adults. In an interview with *Something About the Author*, she said, "For me, historical fiction is the place where story and setting come together. Historical fiction allows all of us, including kids, to look at today's problems through a prism, to get a literal distance on our own problems. I hope my books help kids to see beyond their own experiences, and see themselves as part of the sweep of history instead of an isolated vignette."[1]

After a writer such as Cushman decides to write historical fiction, she still needs to figure out where and when her novels will take place. In an interview with the Internet Public Library, Cushman explained why she likes to write books set in the Middle Ages:

> I like the music, the costumes, the pageantry, and the color. It seems an interesting time, when western civilization was growing towards the Renaissance just like a child growing into

adolescence. I first thought about writing books set in that time after reading about the lives of children in times past. I thought about what it might have been like for them when they had no power and little value. Especially girl children. I wondered how they coped with their lack of value and still kept a sense of their own worth; how they made choices when there were few options; how they survived when they had little power . . . Many children [like Catherine] endured arranged marriages. There were a lot of homeless children [like Brat] at the time and very few people or places to care for them.[2]

Critics esteem that Karen Cushman is one of the most skillful writers of historical fiction within children's literature. This is because she not only creates vivid and historically accurate descriptions of her chosen settings, but because she also writes such realistic and compelling characters.

There are two main kinds of fiction: character-driven and plot-driven. Plot-driven fiction is fiction involving a scintillating, suspenseful, and engaging turn of events, where the characters provide background for the plot. The characters aren't as important because they are only there to react to events happening to or around them. On the other hand, character-driven fiction is where the characters themselves hold the story together, and the plot relies on the characters' personalities and choices rather than a string of unrelated events or coincidences. Without the characters, nothing would happen at all.

There's no doubt which kind of fiction Cushman writes. "I have never been plot-conscious," she said in an interview with *Something About the Author*. "I personally love to read books that have strong plot and strong characters. But when I sit down to write a book, I don't have this structure in mind. I simply want to tell a story about a person's life and how that life changes day to day."[3]

Cushman's novels all confront the familiar adolescent themes of forming identities, taking responsibility, and coming of age. All of her characters share some valuable and admirable characteristics: they are all strong-willed, or stubborn, and find it hard to come to terms with their circumstances; they are all mischievous and feisty, and find it difficult to hold themselves accountable; and they are all in the midst of important life changes, such as figuring out a career or marriage path. Surely, these aspects of life are familiar to young people throughout history.

And why would a writer choose not only to write historical fiction, but to write it for young adults?

In her Newbery Medal acceptance speech for *A Midwife's Apprentice*, she explained these choices:

> "There's worms in apples and worms in radishes," says Arvella Whipple in my newest book. "The worm in the radish, he thinks the whole world is a radish." Those of us who read books know the whole world is not a radish. It is a crabbing boat in the Chesapeake Bay, the walls of medieval Kraków, twenty-first-century Zimbabwe, and the place where the wild things are. It is Narnia and Brooklyn and Gold Rush California. It is the glory of the whirligigs in May's garden, the lonely anger of Heidi's grandfather, the warmth of the wind blowing through the willows, and the terror of a Nazi death camp.
>
> As children are what they eat and hear and experience, so too they are what they read. This is why I write what I do, about strong young women who in one way or another take responsibility for their own lives; about tolerance, thoughtfulness, and caring; about choosing what is life-affirming and generous; about the ways that people are the same and the ways they are different and how rich that makes us all.[4]

The five strong young women Cushman has chosen to portray, Rodzina, Lucy, Catherine, Brat, and Matilda—the heroines of the five lively and skillfully written novels Karen Cushman has written so far—are faced with awesome challenges. These are very different girls living in five very different circumstances. However, each has to learn how to negotiate the circumstances of her life as success-fully as possible. Like people in real life, they don't always succeed in making their deepest desires come true. However, they all manage to find some happiness and peace in their difficult lives. And how do they do it? They do what smart young people in all eras and walks of life must do: use their wits, forge connections with other people, and maintain realistic expectations.

1 Blooming Late

Amelia Earhart, the first woman to fly alone across the Atlantic Ocean, didn't become a famous aviator until she was thirty-five years old. Before learning to fly airplanes, Earhart worked as a file clerk, an English teacher, a photographer, a social worker, a nurse's aid, a fashion designer, and a truck driver.

Another well-known late bloomer is Agatha Christie, whose 100 books established her as the world's best-known mystery writer. Christie didn't publish her first book until she was in her thirties.

Oscar-winning actress Susan Sarandon wasn't famous until she starred in *Bull Durham* in 1988, at age forty. Julia Child, the famous chef, didn't host her first cooking show until she was forty-nine years old. Grandma Moses, one of the most famous folk artists in America, didn't sell her first painting until she was seventy-eight.

"Late bloomer" is a horticultural term that applies to plants that bloom later in life than others. In everyday speech, however, the term refers to people who start their careers or become famous later in life. In previous decades, many women were late bloomers because they had families at a young age, when most men were starting their careers, and then they worked in the home until their kids were grown. Once they had the time, these women started to focus on their careers or passions.

Karen Cushman is a prime example of a late bloomer.

Moving Around

Karen was born to parents Arthur and Loretta Lipski on October 4, 1941, in Chicago, Illinois, just before the United States entered World War II in December of that year. As a young girl, she dreamed of becoming a tap dancer, a movie star, or a librarian. When she was ten years old, her family picked up and moved to Tarzana, California, much to Karen's dismay. Tarzana was small compared to Chicago, and California was too hot for her. Also,

Karen missed her friends and her public library. She had always been an avid reader of anything she could get her hands on, including comic books, Russian novels, books about World War II, and *Mad* magazine, which was a popular young adult comics publication that is still in circulation. Fiction was Karen's favorite genre, but every once in a while, she would have the desire to explore all there was to learn about a certain topic, such as the American Civil War or the physiology of the brain. (As this was her pattern, it's not difficult to imagine how she later became obsessed with learning about the Middle Ages or the gold rush, and then incorporated her knowledge into her novels.) Once she'd found the local library in her new hometown, she felt a little more comfortable. She attended Catholic high school, and unfortunately, at school, she generally felt uneasy about the strictness of the teachers and lack of imagination in her course work.

In her Newbery Medal acceptance speech, Cushman had the following to say about her early home life:

> As a child I wrote constantly but never thought about growing up to be a writer. I come from a working-class Chicago-area family that loved me dearly but often didn't quite know what to make of me. I used to imagine I was the only

child ever kidnapped from gypsies and sold to regular people. I didn't know writing was a job, something real people did with their lives, something like being a secretary, or a salesman, or a school crossing guard, like my grandpa.

With school, writing became hard work—homework assignments, term papers. Like many other students, I procrastinated, suffered, and counted words.

Besides, my greatest passion was not for writing but for reading . . . We didn't own many books; in school I suffered through banal [simplistic] readers, but before long I discovered the library. Then chances were if I could reach it, I would read it.

Writers, I began to think, were people who had all the answers. I didn't have all the answers; I didn't even know all the questions. So I stopped writing, for a very long time, and for years endured the painful search for a place to belong. Some times were great, some empty and awful, but there was always something missing.[1]

The fantasy and imaginative life that Karen missed in her overly controlled school environment was played out at home. She wrote and performed in plays with kids from her neighborhood. Once, she held a ballet class for her friends, teaching them what she'd read in a ballet book. (They held

Writer and Character Converge

It is probably obvious that Karen Cushman is a naturally inquisitive person. During the period when she was researching *Catherine, Called Birdy*, Cushman had been reading a little here and there about saints. She felt that the young character she was writing about was a version of herself, and accordingly, Catherine would most likely be interested in saints. Cushman researched saints and feast days in a book called the *Oxford Dictionary of Saints*.

As Cushman learned in her research, there were more than 25,000 saints by the year 1200—ninety years before the novel takes place. Cushman inserted much of what she learned into Catherine's diary, and many entries begin with a brief explanation of that day's saint. "Feast of Saint Paul of Thebes," Catherine writes on January 20, "the first hermit. He lived to be one hundred and thirteen and two lions dug his grave."[2] Back then, making someone a saint wasn't an official act of the Catholic Church like it is in modern times. The saints Catherine describes in her diary more closely resembled famous historical figures, as we would think of them today, and are no longer officially considered saints. Today, the Catholic Church recognizes only about 10,000 saints.

There is something about the brief descriptions of saints in *Catherine, Called Birdy* that sends the imagination into orbit: Who were these people? Why did their lives turn out so strange and often so violent and tragic? For example, November 28 was the Feast of Saint Juwartha. She wore cheeses on her chest and was beheaded by her stepbrother. May 4 was the Feast of Saint Monica, who overcame a violent husband and a tendency to drink a lot. Catherine doesn't say in her diary how she came to know all she does about the saints of her day. What is clear, though, is that she is as titillated, or excited, by the strange and fascinating stories of these historical figures as Cushman was when she researched them. Like character, like author.

on to the door handles of cars instead of using a bar.) She used to borrow her brother's scooter and take off, imagining herself traveling across the country and the world. She also wrote a lot, mostly poems, short stories, and plays.

In high school, Karen won a scholarship that allowed her to study at any college in the United States. She chose Stanford University, in Palo Alto, California. It was at this time that she started thinking seriously about becoming a writer. "I never thought about writing as a profession or a way to make a living," she said in an interview for *Something About the Author*. "No one I knew made their living that way. I thought I might want to take creative writing in college, but that's as far as the ambition went."[3] Unfortunately for her, at the time Stanford didn't offer undergraduate classes in creative writing. Instead, Karen studied English, Latin, and Greek. She also studied archaeology and fantasized about digging for treasures by moonlight at the Acropolis, the ancient hilltop fortress in Athens, Greece.

Sometimes Dreams Don't Come True (Right Away)

However, the future had less exotic things in store for Karen than treasures in ancient lands. After graduation, Karen worked as a customer service representative at a telephone company in Beverly Hills, California. She bounced from job to job for a few years, and then, when she was twenty-eight years old and working at Hebrew Union College in Los Angeles, she met a rabbinical student named Philip Cushman. They married in 1969. Together, they moved to Oregon so that Philip could work at Lewis and Clark College in Portland. It was there that their daughter, Leah, was born, and Karen took up the hobbies of weaving and making fresh jam. After two years, the Cushmans moved back to California, where they continue to live today with their two dogs and rabbit.

Philip and Karen both attended graduate school at the United States International University and received degrees in counseling and human behavior in 1977. Philip went on to get his doctorate in human psychology. Meanwhile, Karen went back to school for a second master's degree. This time she attended John F. Kennedy University and in 1986 earned a degree in museum studies, which enabled her to research artifacts and design museum exhibits. After she graduated, she stayed at the school to teach classes in museum studies and to edit the school's *Museum Studies Journal*.

In an interview, Cushman explained her interest in the field: "Museum studies was an interesting way for me to put together many of the things that interested me in life. I am fascinated about the concept of what artifacts say about a culture, and also which artifacts are saved and why others are not."[4]

Meanwhile, a large part of the time spent with her daughter involved reading children's books. When Leah reached the age when she was reading young adult novels, Cushman realized that she, too, really enjoyed this genre. When Leah moved on to adult books, Cushman didn't want to stop reading about the young adult characters and situations she cared about and had been fascinated with for so many years. She was compelled with the themes of young adult novels: coming of age, accepting responsibility, and becoming aware of identity. She eventually started to develop ideas of her own for young adult novels, and she always shared these ideas with her husband. Then, one day in 1989 when Cushman was forty-seven years old, she told her husband about an idea for a story about a girl living in the Middle Ages. His response was that he didn't want to hear about another idea unless she actually wrote it down. As Cushman had been talking about writing for many years, it seemed that it was time for her to stop talking about it and start doing it. In her Newbery Medal acceptance speech, she recalled the time when she committed herself to authoring books, at long last:

> Finally, the day my daughter began filling out college applications, I sat down to write, for myself. I still didn't have the answers, but I began to know some of the questions: Why? What for? What if? How would it be?

> Writing was still hard work—hard to begin, hard to stop. But it also became a passion, and that made all the difference. "To sum it all up," Ray Bradbury [a famous science-fiction writer] said,

"if you want to write, if you want to create, you must be the most sublime fool that God ever turned out and sent rambling . . . I wish for you a wrestling match with your creative muse that will last a lifetime. I wish craziness and foolishness and madness upon you. May you live with hysteria, and out of it make fine stories . . . Which finally means, may you be in love every day for the next 20,000 days and out of that love, remake the world."

I read that, and I said, "Yes." And out of my passion came *Catherine, Called Birdy*, my first book. I wrote it despite my own doubts and the "don'ts" of others, because I needed to find out about things, about identity and responsibility, compassion and kindness and belonging, and being human in the world. How could I learn them if I couldn't write about them?

Sometime during the process of writing *Catherine*, I thought of the title *The Midwife's Apprentice*. I liked it. So I made a file. I wrote *The Midwife's Apprentice* on the tab. Inside I wrote on a slip of paper, "Possible title—*Midwife's Apprentice*." And I filed it.[5]

In an interview with the *News Tribune* of Tacoma, Washington, Cushman further explained why she chose this time in her life to begin writing novels. She said, "When Leah was in her last year of high school I felt like this psychic space was opening up in my head. It's that space that was filled with, 'Does she have her lunch money? What is she doing this weekend? Who's driving?' All those questions were going out, and I had room for other questions, like 'What if there was this girl . . . ?'"[6]

It took her three years of painstaking research, but eventually, the idea became her first novel, *Catherine, Called Birdy*. By this time, it was clear that a late bloomer had definitely bloomed.

Girls as Inspiration

In addition to falling in love with the books Leah read as an adolescent, Cushman was moved to write young adult fiction for her daughter and her daughter's adolescent friends. She dedicated her first novel, in fact, "to Leah, Danielle, Megan, Molly, Pamela, and Tama, and to the imagination, hope, and tenacity [perseverance] of all young women."[7] In her 1996 Newbery Medal acceptance speech (for *The Midwife's Apprentice*), Cushman thanked her daughter for showing her "every day how strong and independent yet gentle and compassionate a young woman can be."[8]

Cushman told *Something About the Author*, "I don't consciously think of the audience as I am writing, and I certainly do not wonder if the vocabulary level is correct or not. I just tell a story the way it has to be told."[9] In an interview with the *San Francisco Chronicle*, she explained that she was interested in what people typically consider adolescent issues, such as coming of age, forming new identities, taking responsibility—the themes that show up again and again in her novels. And she simply prefers writing about young girls rather than grown-ups. "I know adult books deal with heavy stuff, too," she said, "but you can count on books for children or young adults to leave you with some hope, even if they don't have a happy ending."[10]

2 Introducing Catherine, Alyce, Matilda, Lucy, and Rodzina

Reading about Catherine, Alyce, Matilda, Lucy, and Rodzina is like traveling backward to times and places that one does not usually visit in many young adult novels. However, what makes Cushman such a skilled writer is that you don't have to know anything about the Middle Ages to appreciate the life and times of the three bright, caring, stubborn, and lively girls who are the main protagonists in her work.

Catherine

As mentioned, Catherine, the main character of *Catherine, Called Birdy*, is a feisty and headstrong adolescent girl living with her family (as well as with lots of other people, servants, and travelers) in a manor in an English village in the year 1290. She dreams of winning an argument against her parents over the matter of her arranged marriage and about her desire to dress like a boy and fight in the Crusades, which were expeditions meant to spread Christianity into other parts of the world. After more than a year of writing in her diary about the various people and difficulties she has encountered in her life, Catherine finally reaches an age-old (but nonetheless difficult) realization: she can run, but she can't hide.

Catherine's story is told through a series of journal entries in which she describes her village, friends, suitors, and the hijinks she's involved with in vivid detail. Some readers might feel that her circumstances, including her arranged marriage, are sad and limiting. Regardless of the somber subject matter, Catherine's humor and spirit keep the novel fast-paced and engaging.

Community and Hierarchy in the Middle Ages

As Cushman points out in the author's note at the back of *Catherine, Called Birdy*, 1290s England was very different from the contemporary England we think of today. However, there are similarities as well as differences. For example, Middle English, which was spoken from roughly the twelfth through fifteenth centuries, shares a similar sentence structure with Modern English, though many spellings, expressions, and verb tenses differ. If you read a book written in Middle English (without opting for a modernized version), you might understand every third or fourth sentence, and generally, you would be able to follow the story. Similarly, if you attended a celebration or festival that took place in the Middle Ages, you would recognize many activities from modern-day parties—dancing, for example, and eating and drinking (though at the time children were allowed to drink alcohol as well as adults). People's homes, too, were not completely unlike modern homes, though manors were much bigger and housed more people, not just one family.

One particular characteristic of people in the Middle Ages was that they were very tied to their communities. Where a person was born was part of who that person was—a part of his or her identity. Very few people aspired to leave their villages, unless they were part of the Crusades. Even those who went to fight in the Crusades always returned to their hometowns.

People were divided into a hierarchy, or ranking. The king at the top, followed by dukes, barons, and counts. After that were the knights and abbots. At the bottom were the farmers, blacksmiths, and other villagers. Land was divided along class lines. The king owned everything within England and rented out large plots of it to barons, counts, and dukes. In turn, they rented out smaller sections to knights and abbots, who rented out even smaller sections of their property to regular villagers. This way, the less powerful people paid rent to those above them, who paid rent to those above them, and so on, until the king was paid. Landlords became responsible for their renters and needed to protect them and keep them safe. This meant that everyone in the entire country was connected to each other—from the king to the smallest landholder.

In the novel *Catherine, Called Birdy*, Catherine's father is a knight. He owns one manor and enough land to support his family. He rents out parcels of land to the villagers in his town in exchange for goods or services. Every so often, he throws festivals and feasts during which everyone in the village gets together at the manor. In 1290, a typical village consisted of one road leading from the manor to a church, which every villager attended. The road would be lined with small cottages, and of course, everyone knew everybody else.

Alyce

Brat, the main character in Cushman's Newbery-Medal–winning novel, *The Midwife's Apprentice*, has Catherine's feistiness and humor, though she is in perhaps even more difficult circumstances. She, too, lives in medieval England, though not in a manor, and not surrounded by family and villagers.

The narrative begins with Brat lying in a garbage heap to keep warm and proceeds through her introduction to a snaggletoothed midwife named Jane Sharp. Brat becomes Jane's apprentice, though she starts out failing more often than delivering. Although Brat is basically nameless at the start of her journey (since no one knows her well enough to even call her by name), Jane calls her Brat, then briefly Beetle. Then, as Brat's character develops and she grows more self-confident, she acquires the name Alyce, which becomes her name for good. She begins her life as an apprentice playing tricks on villagers who had been mean to her, but then she ends up taking her destiny into her own hands and acting instead of reacting. She learns to read and finds herself a new job, which ends up bringing her back where she belongs, working as a midwife. Eventually, Alyce comes to understand that to be successful, she must apply herself instead of running away from her troubles.

Cushman described Alyce in her own words in her 1996 Newbery Medal acceptance speech:

> Children ask me who Alyce is—is she me or someone I know? Alyce is Alyce, a girl with no place in a world all about place, a girl who has to give birth to herself. And I am Alyce, who becomes truly alive only when she learns to smile and sing and tell stories to the cat. You are Alyce, if only in the way that all of us are, born cold and nameless, in search of a full belly and a place in this world. And Alyce is every child who is parentless, homeless, and hungry, who lives on the edges of our world, who is mocked or excluded for being different.[1]

Matilda

Matilda, who was born into a wealthy family, suffers because her mother left soon after her birth and her father died when she was a young child. At the start of *Matilda Bone*, Matilda's guardian, Father Leufredus, has just abandoned her—he literally dropped her at the front door of a local bonesetter named Peg. His intention was that Matilda, who is fourteen years old at the time, become an apprentice. However, unfortunately for Matilda, she is disgusted by her new surroundings and by Peg, whom she looks down upon because Peg is uneducated and seems uncouth. As the plot continues, Matilda comes to

Education in the Middle Ages

In the Middle Ages, children were schooled at home and taught whatever their parents could teach them. For example, if you were the son of sheep-herders, you learned to herd sheep. Some children became apprentices, or assistants, to craftspeople, millers (people who operated grain mills), or black-smiths. Young women, especially those who had noble parents, were taught sewing and embroidery, music, and good social manners in preparation for marriage. This allowed for villages to maintain a certain way of life generation after generation. If young people grew up and left home for distant places, what would happen to the village? Eventually, there would be no one to mill the grain, or make horseshoes, or tend the sheep. The villagers' entire way of life would unravel and ultimately cease to exist. Fortunately, this didn't happen because of the loyalty people felt to their hometowns.

realize that the education she has previously received has little to do with helping people in her new life. Ultimately, she learns that to become a better person, she must learn to accept her surroundings and Peg's unfamiliar teachings.

Medicine in the Middle Ages

In *Matilda Bone*, Matilda and Peg attempt to straighten people's broken bones without having the benefit of modern science or surgery. Today, when people break their legs, their legs can be reset by a doctor in a hospital, or if people have poor eyesight, they can be fitted for glasses or contact lenses. Imagine if these things were not possible—people with broken legs would never heal and would have trouble walking for the rest of their lives, and people with poor eyesight would just not be able to see.

Medicine is especially important in Cushman's books because much of the time, girls and women were in charge of healing (even though they were not often considered doctors). The woman of the manor was generally the one who healed cuts and bruises for the townspeople—so Catherine, as the daughter of the manor, was also expected to be able to attend to minor medical injuries. At the time, medicine, which had been the same for hundreds of years, consisted mostly of herbal remedies, most of which were ineffective.

In *Matilda Bone*, medieval medicine is explored in detail. This kind of information about something foreign to modern adolescents is a big part of what makes Cushman's novels so interesting and engaging. Cushman has said in interviews that she has one thing in common with eighth-grade kids: she relishes things that are kind of gross.

In fact, Cushman enjoyed the medical details so much that *Matilda Bone* originally read a little like a textbook on medieval medicine—that was how much information found its way into her first draft. Even though much of that information was ultimately cut, Cushman found room for the more scintillating details. In the author's note at the back of the novel, she explains medieval medicine to the reader: "We who are accustomed to modern doctors and practices might not even recognize medieval medicine as medicine."[2]

Indeed, people of the era believed in what might be called witchcraft, or at least old wives' tales: charms, incantations (songs or spells), relics (artifacts from the past, usually having some important meaning), devils, fairies, gnomes (ageless dwarfs who guard treasure), flying witches, and the power of a unicorn's horn. Some "doctors" used leeches or cut veins to let excess blood leave the body, thereby balancing the "humors," or fluids, in the body. It was believed that these fluids needed to be balanced in order to promote good health. Some healers thought that many illnesses were a result of worms entering the body. While soap existed, there was little or no attention paid to the benefits of what is now known as standard nutrition and hygiene.

During the Middle Ages, no one knew about the existence of germs and bacteria or the transmission of disease. This doesn't mean there was no such thing as medicine, but modern-day physicians might not recognize medieval cures as such today. Apothecaries, or pharmacists, prescribed and sold snail shells, raven dung, herbs, broth made from the rags of Egyptian mummies, poppies, foxglove, bread mold, and so on. Penicillin had not yet been invented and eyeglasses wouldn't be developed until the late fourteenth century.

Also, because people were usually taught by apprenticeship instead of schooling, and villages were small, one person might end up working multiple jobs. For example, a barber-surgeon might be responsible for cutting hair, pulling teeth, treating wounds, and amputating limbs, all with limited knowledge and few tools. As a result of this lack of concentrated study or knowledge, most diseases ended up being fatal, and most surgeries were failures.

At one point in *Matilda Bone*, Matilda, who has not yet realized that some healers don't need Latin or sophisticated education to be effective, visits the great Master Theobald. He is the most respected physician in the village, and Matilda seeks the master's advice for her friend Nathaniel, who is losing his eyesight. The physician sends her back and forth between his home and Nathaniel's, seeking more and more seemingly irrelevant information. For example, questions such as, Where and when was Nathaniel born? What time of the year did the eyesight troubles start? What dreams has Nathaniel had lately? Were any of the dreams about toothaches or floods? In the end, Master Theobald charges more than Matilda and Nathaniel can pay and he does nothing to help Nathaniel's eyesight.

Eventually, Matilda comes to understand what Peg and her friends already know: that wisdom and kindness don't always come with higher education and degrees, but are sometimes more important to the healing process.

Lucy

In the novel *The Ballad of Lucy Whipple* (1996), Lucy, the twelve-year-old protagonist, and her widowed mother have moved to a mining town in California. This was during the 1840s, when people from all across America moved west hoping to strike it rich by mining gold. Lucy finds herself homesick, confused, and in the way. Ultimately, she's not very pleased. "You said we'd find our fortunes," she tells her mother, "but I don't see any gold. Only rocks and holes and lizards."[3] Lucy ends up cooking and cleaning for the tenants of her mother's boarding house and sleeping in a tent. She desperately misses all the things that used to be familiar to her: school, friends, libraries. (This is very similar to the way Cushman felt when she was a young girl and her family moved from Chicago to California.) Her new surroundings are little more, in her eyes, than a bunch of tents and some down-on-their-luck miners—and there's no lending library there at all. She vows to make it back to New England at any cost and to hate California in the meantime; she even invents a scheme to sell pies to earn her passage back. But something strange happens, something unexpected: Lucy starts to feel more and more at home in the mining town, and luckier and luckier even though there is no gold to be found. Lucy is forced to make a new, fulfilling life for herself, and when given the opportunity to return to her comfortable New England hometown, she declines it.

A Brief History of the Gold Rush

Back in the 1840s, much of the area that makes up the present-day United States was still largely unsettled. Only a handful of people had managed to make it all the way westward to California. Early in the 1840s, San Francisco, now a metropolis of nearly three-quarters of a million people, was home to only a few hundred residents.

In 1839, a wealthy Swiss immigrant named John Sutter moved to California to escape his financial troubles in his home country. In the course of building a sawmill, his outfit discovered gold. Slowly, word of the discovery spread to the general American population. By 1848, with the help of President James Polk, gold fever had reached the East Coast, and people prepared to move westward hoping to make their fortunes. The year of the great move westward was 1849. It's because of this that those who went west during the gold rush became known as forty-niners.

Cushman was fascinated by the gold rush, but more specifically, she was extremely intrigued by one fact she had heard: 90 percent of the people who went west during the gold rush were men. What about that other 10 percent? she asked herself. Where were the women and children? Why did they come? What did they find? Were they happy? Did they choose to move west, or did they have no choice in the matter? Cushman found her answers by immersing herself in studying the history of the era. Ultimately, all of her research became a novel.

Rodzina

Like many of her novels, Cushman's fifth and most recent book, *Rodzina* (2003), places a heroine in an unlikely and unfamiliar setting. This time, readers are transported to 1881 as an orphan train is leaving Chicago. An orphan train was a train that delivered dozens of children, ranging in age from newborns to adolescents, to the West to find new homes—though many of them were adopted into lives of hard labor and slavery. Rodzina—whose full name is Rodzina Clara Jadwiga Anastazya Brodski—is a Polish immigrant whose family has fallen upon hard times. Her younger brother was killed in a house fire, her father was killed in the slaughterhouse where he worked, and her mother died of grief. All of this tragedy left twelve-year-old Rodzina with only a few trinkets and a desolate-looking future.

Rodzina has no option but to live on the streets. She does this until a police officer takes her to the orphan train.

From the moment Rodzina boards the orphan train, her journey becomes more difficult. Cushman describes in enthralling detail the harsh conditions on the orphan train. For example, a coal stove is used for heat, and wooden benches are the only things on which these orphans can sleep.

A Brief History of the Orphan Train

In 1853, maps were drawn for the purpose of building new railroad lines across America. To advertise this incredible feat of engineering, the U.S. government distributed posters, fliers, and other advertisements not only around the country but also in Europe and the rest of the Western world. This international advertising campaign heralded the United States as the "land of milk and honey." Europeans were led to believe that if they left their homes and settled in the United States, they would be all but guaranteed a life filled with easily obtained wealth.

As a result of all of this advertising, more immigrants came to the United States than at any other time in history, including the time of the pilgrims, who settled the original British colonies. Almost overnight, cities became too crowded and the rate of homelessness rose dramatically. More and more people were unemployed because everyone was desperate for work and would accept very low wages. This was before child labor laws, hence, even young children were working to help support their families. Many people died from living in overcrowded and unsanitary environments. Of course, this meant that many children lost one or both parents, and accordingly more and more orphanages needed to be built.

In 1853, in order to help place orphans and homeless kids with families, a man named Charles Loring Brace founded the Children's Aid Society of New York. The society's representatives visited towns along the orphan train's route and interviewed families who were willing to take in children. The train was a less expensive way to transport children to new homes. Between 1854 and 1929, as a result of the orphan train, hundreds of thousands of children were placed with rural American families. Some historians estimate that there were as many as 350,000 children on the trains.

The Children's Aid Society was confident that good, loving homes could be found for all the orphans—but often this was far from the case. Many families were simply looking for help for the immense labor that was needed for the overwhelming farm work with which they were confronted. As such, they treated the orphans as hired help at best. Many children were abused by their new parents, and some were ultimately turned out onto the street when they dared to express displeasure with their slavelike status. However, many success stories also occurred. For example, two street boys named Andrew Burke and John Brady, who were placed on the orphan train and put in loving homes, grew up to be governors of their states (North Dakota and Alaska, respectively).

When Charles Loring Brace, the founder of the Children's Aid Society, died in 1890, he was remembered as the most important children's rights worker in the nineteenth century. Eventually, things started changing for children in America—society was placing less and less importance on the virtue of hard work, and more and more on the value of play and happiness. It was becoming more important to adult society that kids were psychologically happy, and this didn't fit with the orphan train's emphasis on placing children with families who would feed them in return for their labor.

The last orphan train took three boys to a home in Sulphur Springs, Texas, on May 31, 1929. To this day, there continue to be annual reunions between orphan train riders and their children, grandchildren, and great-grandchildren all over the United States.

For food, they have to make do with cold sandwiches. Through the narrative voice of Rodzina, Cushman describes anguishing scenes, such as how at each stop, the children are made to stand on the platform to be inspected by potential parents.

At one stop, Rodzina is approached by two elderly sisters who ask the orphans' chaperone, the adult traveling with them, if Rodzina is strong enough to carry a hundred-pound (forty-five-kilogram) sack of flour and if she is good at washing feet and emptying chamber pots. This gives Rodzina—and the reader—a chilling idea of what might await her if she goes with the women. Meanwhile, another man on the platform is interested in Rodzina—not as a daughter, however (he already has thirteen children), but as a wife. He needs someone who can cook, clean, and take care of him. Rodzina can't stand to think of what her life would be like with these possible "families." However, she has no other options, or at least it doesn't seem like she does. Rodzina tries living in a few different homes but ends up living with the orphans' chaperone, a woman as lonely and lost as Rodzina herself.

Rodzina's greatest wish is for a loving, supportive family and home. Her desires and needs are very simple: she wants to live somewhere where she can come home from school and do homework on the kitchen table. Although this is not an outrageous desire, for her it seems like an impossible dream.

3 Bringing Characters and Places to Life

The five main characters that Cushman has drawn so vividly (Alyce, Catherine, Matilda, Lucy, and Rodzina) are ultimately able to take some control of their difficult lives. However, this only occurs once they realize that they have the ability to use their own talents and interests to help them forge a better future. For example, Alyce uses her natural curiosity and excellent memory to become a better apprentice; Catherine learns when being stubborn can be a useful trait and that, ultimately, she has to accept her arranged marriage as it's the only way that she might have a calmer and happier future. Matilda uses her love of scholarship and learning to write letters and study medicine.

Cushman's heroines don't have every available option open to them. Nonetheless, when they open themselves up to the breadth of their situations, it turns out that they do have more control over their lives than it seems—regardless of the difficult circumstances of their home lives.

Readers and critics of Cushman's works are continually impressed by how clearly and vividly she is able to convey her characters and their settings. Basically, accomplishing this involves intense research, sophisticated and highly honed writing skills, and a highly sensitive and intuitive understanding of various themes or life problems that are ultimately shared by all adolescents, regardless of the time period.

Turning History into Story

It's not easy to learn about a time period and place you've never experienced and then write about it with such convincing authenticity and clarity that readers are able to relate to events and circumstances that are completely foreign to them. In order to realistically re-create a place and time period, an author can't just have a general idea about it— he or she has to know it in detail. This entails having specific knowledge of what people wore, how they spoke, what sort of things concerned them, what delighted them, what routines they maintained, what they ate, and other such questions.

Cushman is one of dozens of young adult authors who write historical fiction; however, her work stands out in terms of how compelling and authentic she is able to render the characters she creates. Consider this passage from *Catherine, Called Birdy*, which, as mentioned previously, is written in the form of a medieval girl's diary:

> The stars and my family align to make my life black and miserable. My mother seeks to make me a fine lady—dumb, docile [obedient], and accomplished—so I must take lady-lessons and keep my mouth closed. My brother Edward thinks even girls should not be ignorant, so he taught me to read holy books and to write, even though I would rather sit in an apple tree and wonder. Now my father, the toad, conspires [plots] to sell me like a cheese to some lack-wit seeking a wife.
>
> What makes this clodpole [blockhead] suitor anxious to have me? I am no beauty, being sun-browned and gray-eyed, with poor eyesight and stubborn disposition. My family holds but two small manors. We have plenty of cheese and apples but no silver or jewels or boundless acres to attract a suitor.
>
> Corpus bones! He comes to dine with us in two days' time. I plan to cross my eyes and drool in my meat.[1]

It's partially Cushman's use of time-appropriate vocabulary that makes this passage ring with such authenticity. Words such as "clodpole suitor," "lack-wit," and "lady-lessons" are not common to modern readers, but the context in which the characters utter them nonetheless renders them comprehensible even to an unaccustomed ear.

"Corpus bones," an exclamation from the Middle Ages, would never be heard today. It basically means "Darn it!" There's a certain formal way of speaking that Cushman has captured in Catherine's voice, and it comes across throughout the novel—as though Cushman were literally able to travel through time and slip into the body of an adolescent girl living in an English manor in the Middle Ages. To accomplish this kind of seemingly flawless sense of realism, a writer must do a tremendous amount of hard work before even writing the first word. Of course, all of this detailed intensive work falls under the heading of research.

Blood, Sweat, and Tons of Books

When it comes to research, Cushman is a very methodical person as well as being very organized. First, she reads some of the better-known writers of historical fiction for young adults. For example, she has read works by Patricia MacLachlan, who wrote *Sarah, Plain and Tall* (1985), which is set on a

Midwestern homestead in the nineteenth century. Cushman has also read the works of Rosemary Sutcliff, who sets most of her novels during the Roman Empire's occupation of Britain in the years AD 125 to 425 (long before the Middle Ages). She felt that both writers were excellent models for the type of in-depth historical research she wanted to use in her novels. The prose style, clean and polished, of their historical fiction was exactly the style she was seeking for her own writing.

Armed with her museum experience and love of young adult novels, Cushman set about learning what it was like to be a young girl in England in the Middle Ages. She read a lot—not just books about the period but also primary sources, or firsthand accounts, such as letters and diaries. Other primary sources she examined were cookbooks and books on etiquette dating from the period. She also read secondary sources, or written materials that date from much later than the period. The subjects of these sources ranged from clothing to agriculture to lifestyle of the Middle Ages.

As Cushman explained in an interview in the *News Tribune*, "I figured out that what they were telling people not to do in the 14th century were probably the things they were doing, things like not blowing your nose on the tablecloth, and not putting chewed meat into the common bowl."[2] She then transferred these examples of the poorly behaved people (for example, drunks and unappealing suitors in *Catherine, Called Birdy*) into her novels.

Cushman spent hours upon hours and weeks upon weeks sorting through sources in order to discover what it was like to live in the Middle Ages. Some of the basic information she was looking for was to answer questions such as, What did people eat? What were their daily routines? How did they go to the bathroom without modern plumbing? What were their names?

In an interview on the Internet Public Library, a Web site where readers can find information about their favorite authors and books, Cushman said:

> For *Catherine* and *The Midwife's Apprentice*, I learned all about bee-keeping, shearing sheep, ointments and remedies, superstitions and fears, clothing, food, language, table manners, bathing habits, and privies [bathrooms]. But just as important, if not more, I researched ideas, attitudes, assumptions, values, expectations. They have changed since ages past. I tried very hard to make the books realistic and truthful about the Middle Ages. Medieval people were different from us.[3]

Cushman has said that although she loves to read, writing provides her with a much greater sense of accomplishment, especially because so much research goes into each of her books. Typically—as Cushman divulged in an interview with students on AuthorChats (www.authorchats.com), a Web site devoted to putting young readers in contact with their favorite authors, she spends one to two years writing a rough draft, and only then does "the real work begin."[4]

Of course, a large percentage of what Cushman learned during her intense research never found its way into her books—or at least hasn't made it into a book yet.

Some people might not consider reading to be an experience that expands the horizons, especially when so many books are set in familiar times and places. Books about young adults in the Middle Ages introduce readers to the mysteries of life in past times as well as provide them with a broader and more encompassing perspective on the experience of adolescence throughout time. How can a reader not be humbled by the fact that his or her concerns and joys have been felt by adolescents across the world for hundreds of years?

Painting a Picture

Cushman puts almost as much effort into describing the physical appearances of all her characters as she does into researching their eras and settings.

For example, when Catherine writes in her diary, she explains to the reader what her friend Perkin looks like. She says, "Although he is the goat boy, Perkin is my good friend and heart's brother. He is very thin and goodly looking with golden hair and blue eyes just like the king, but is much dirtier than the king although much cleaner than other villagers."[5] It's not easy to convey a character's looks to the reader, especially when a novel is written like a diary. However, Cushman's novels are always brimming with vividly painted images that ultimately end up enriching the reader's experience.

An example of Cushman's use of realistic character description occurs when Matilda first meets her new employer, Peg, who is the bonesetter on Blood and Bone Alley. At this point in the novel, Matilda has just been dropped off by the priest who raised her from infancy.

Matilda [peered] at her new mistress in the dim light: hair orange as a carrot peeping from beneath a greasy handkerchief; a big smile that showed more spaces than teeth, although she appeared of no great age yet; and a face beslobbered with freckles, forehead to chin, ear to ear; tall and lean, plain, common, and most ill-mannered. Not fine and saintly—but no hair moles, either.[6]

In addition to vividly describing characters to readers, many writers give their characters something memorable or special for which to be known. This descriptive technique helps leave an impression with the reader. For example, Matilda is the only one in her story, and one of very few people in her time period, who can read and write in English and Latin. Another example of a memorable characteristic is that Catherine keeps birds in cages in her chamber, or bedroom.

Shared Themes

Though each of Cushman's novels introduces readers to a different time period or a particular era of historical importance within a given time period, they have a lot in common. In each of her novels, Cushman examines the life of an adolescent girl in a different time period. All of her main protagonists are smart, resourceful, and stubborn. In addition to these similarities, all of Cushman's books examine a few shared themes.

- **Taking Responsibility**

  It's not easy to hold yourself accountable for mistakes you've made, whether it's something you said or did, or an error in your thinking. In *The Midwife's Apprentice*, Alyce must decide whether a mistake she's made was just that—an isolated error—or if it's symbolic of a deep-seated deficiency. And this could mean that she's not cut out to be a midwife, which is what she has hoped to become.

In *Matilda Bone*, Matilda must come to terms with the fact that life isn't anything like what she's learned from books. She has difficulty in accepting the fact that people can be intelligent and helpful even if they don't have the ability to read and write in Latin. She also learns not to be so rigid and that, usually, there is always more than one way to get things done. Hence, she is confronted with her need to be more flexible and forgiving.

- **Knowing When to Give In**

  As mentioned, all the adolescent protagonists of Cushman's novels are stubborn by nature. This means that when someone has an idea about something, he or she doesn't easily let go of it. Catherine, for example, is determined not to marry any of the suitors her father has chosen for her. Eventually, though, she must come to terms with the responsibilities of her birthright and accept her situation. This is especially true when her acceptance enables her to do some good for someone else. For someone who is very headstrong, it's not easy to give in, but ultimately, she comes to realize that this is what she must do.

- ## Forming New Identities

  Like many young women today, Cushman's characters often have nicknames that seem appropriate when they are younger but no longer suit them once they reach a certain level of maturity. For example, Lucy Whipple's given name was California, but once her mother moves her to the state after which she was named, she decides to change it to Lucy. In a letter to her grandparents back East, she says that she cannot hate California and be California. Brat insists on renaming herself Alyce once her life on the streets is finished. And Catherine—who is already called Birdy because of her fondness for birds—later wants to be known as Aelgifu. Aelgifu was the wife of an English king from the eleventh century. The name means "noble gift" and is also spelled Eligifu. By accepting her given name, Catherine is able to come to terms with her birthright and the circumstances that result from that. Matilda comes to accept the last name, Bone, that seems to attach itself to her once her apprenticeship as a bonesetter is under way. In doing so, Matilda claims the future she once stubbornly refused to accept.

The Problem of Happy Endings

During the Middle Ages, the role of young women in the family and society was very different from what it is at present and, more specifically, in terms of what a young woman could hope to achieve. This is perhaps most true in Catherine's life, since she represents the squandered talent of girls who, back in the thirteenth century, were sold like cattle into arranged marriages and forced to look and behave according to strict standards.

Through the character of Catherine, Cushman has made an important statement about how far women have come in society and how hard it must have been for earlier generations. The following passage from Catherine's diary sums up a woman's role during the era, and Catherine's attitude toward that role:

> It is impossible to do all and be all a lady must be and not tie oneself in a knot. A lady must walk erect with dignity, looking straight before her

with eyelids low, gazing at the ground ahead, neither trotting nor running nor looking about nor laughing nor stopping to chatter . . .

She must not show anger, nor sulk, nor scold, nor overeat, nor overdrink, nor swear. God's thumbs! I am going out to the barn to jump, fart, and pick my teeth![7]

The problem Cushman was forced to confront in her writing was this: most heroines in young adult novels must figure a way to solve their problems for themselves, thereby coming of age by the end of the book. However, Catherine's situation is unsolvable—she simply cannot escape her circumstances, and she must learn to live with the fact that her marriage will be arranged. So, how does an author write a compelling story in which the protagonist matures without being untrue to the facts of life of that period? Cushman wanted to show with Catherine what an adolescent might do in a terrible, uncontrollable situation, one in which she had few options and no power.

This is not nearly as simple as it sounds, of course. In her efforts not to be married off to various suitors, Catherine tries to pass herself off as a lunatic and even sets fire to the privy with one suitor still in it. She manages to scare most of the suitors away, except for one formidable suitor whom she has named Shaggy Beard. Only after she has exhausted all the tricks up her sleeve must she confront the reality of her situation and find a way to come to terms with it. She comes to understand that she has certain important obligations and that not fulfilling those obligations will leave her alone and without the support of her community.

The conflict Cushman confronts leaves little room for a happy ending, which is a challenge every good writer must face head-on. Eventually, Catherine must accept her fate, and it is Cushman's job as a writer to show how Catherine does this without being terribly depressed or abandoning her principles.

Adolescence Through the Ages

Many fiction writers make use of the characters they create to explore their lives as though they, the writers themselves, were living it. Cushman readily admits to living vicariously through her female protagonists, even if the time periods and circumstances they live in are very different from Cushman's own childhood. As she noted in an interview with HarperCollins, "I think I make the girls the way I wish I had been." She continued, "They're somewhat like me but they're more independent and outgoing."[8]

The Middle Ages: A Timeline

395 Theodosius leaves the Roman Empire to his two sons, who divide the empire into the West and East.

405 The sons are weak rulers, and many Roman generals revolt. An English general declares himself emperor and then leads armies in a march on Rome. This marks the end of Rome's control of Britain.

520 The first monastery is established in Italy.

600 Around this time, people outside of England begin to invade its borders because the Romans are no longer present. By the middle of the century, England is in the control of the Anglo-Saxons, who came from Germany.

800 Charlemagne is crowned king of the Holy Roman Empire by the pope. Charlemagne's rule symbolizes the official combination of the powers of the Catholic Church and the government. He is considered the most powerful ruler of the Roman Empire.

1066 William the Conqueror invades England and defeats Harold to become king.

1095 The First Crusade begins. Crusaders were Christians from all over Europe who fought throughout the twelfth, thirteenth, and fourteenth centuries to recover the Holy Land from the Muslims.

1099 Crusaders capture Jerusalem.

1147 The Second Crusade begins.

1189 The Third Crusade begins.

1202 The Fourth Crusade begins.

1215 King John of England signs the Magna Carta. This important document states that the king is not above the law.

1291 The Crusades end.

1337 The Hundred Years' War breaks out between England and France when King Edward III tries to claim his right to rule France.

1348 The black plague sweeps through England and Europe. Approximately one of every five people in England dies from the plague. The plague doesn't end until 1351.

1431 During the Hundred Years' War, a young French girl becomes a powerful military leader and earns herself the title Joan of Arc. In 1431, however, the English capture Joan of Arc and burn her at the stake.

1455 After the Hundred Years' War ends, civil war breaks out in England over the question of who gets to be king; this series of wars is called the Wars of the Roses.

1485 The Wars of the Roses finally end, and Henry VII takes control of England. Henry VII dismantles the rule of the aristocracy and leads to the eventual end of the feudal system.

> **1500** What is now known as the Middle Ages comes to an end. The church has become weaker as a result of internal conflicts and conflicts with the government. The feudal system has been weakened by the Hundred Years' War, and the notion of a modern state, with a separation of government and religion and pursuit of intellectualism and culture, begins to become more popular.

In creating characters that are rendered so authentic to present-day readers, Cushman is drawing parallels between the challenges her heroines face and challenges young adults face today. Everyone is forced into certain circumstances, and sometimes these circumstances are extremely challenging. For example, many people are still born into poverty, abusive homes, or communities where they are not free to express themselves as they wish they could.

The actions and words of Cushman's main protagonists illustrate that having a strong will does not mean rebelling and running away. Instead, it means learning what one can learn or gain from a given challenge, and using this knowledge and awareness to become a stronger and more self-aware person. This is not an easy task. Cushman's characters must speak up when they aren't asked to and find creative ways to fix their own problems, when often it would be easier to just continue to be unhappy in the situation as it is. In real life, people often have no choice where or with whom they live, but they have many more choices than they realize when it comes to how they mature and what kind of people they become. Even when the situation seems hopeless, the characters Cushman has created manage to find a way to persevere, as can modern-day young people who find themselves overwhelmed by their circumstances.

This is a very important message for readers.

4 A Writer's Life

Normally a private person, Cushman revealed more about her reasons for wanting to be a writer in her Newbery Honor acceptance speech of 1996 when she was recognized in the children's literature community for *Catherine, Called Birdy*. As she stated in the speech:

> Among native Australian people, it is said, when the rice crop shows sign of failure, the women go into the rice field, bend down, and relate to it the history of its origins; the rice, now understanding why it is there, begins again to grow.

> Aha, I thought, as I read this passage, such is the importance of stories. This is why I write.

I don't start a book by thinking of the listener or the reader; I just climb inside a story and write it over and over again until I know what it's about. Then I try to write as clearly and honestly as I can.

But when the book is finished and I hold it in my hands, I can see myself bending down to whisper it into the ear of a child. You are there, too—you writers, illustrators, booksellers, publishers, and librarians, all whispering away. And the child, now understanding, begins to grow. This is why I write—so children can begin to grow, to see beyond the edges of their own experience.

There are other reasons, also, why I write—not quite so philosophical and high-minded. I write because it's something I can do at home barefoot; because I can lie on my bed and read and call it work; because I am always making up stories in my head anyway and I might as well make a living from them; because I am fifty-four years old and I just figured out that I am not immortal. Like Jacqueline Woodson, I want to leave a sign of having been here. I have ideas, opinions, things to say, and I want to say them before I go. I want to take sides, to argue from my own passions and values and beliefs. I have questions I want to explore in an attempt to find, with Herb Gardner, "the subtle, sneaky important reason" I was born a human being and not a chair.

But maybe, most of all, I write because when I relax and trust myself, it feels so right to be a writer. Writing is my niche, my home, my place in the world, a place I finally found, just as Alyce, *The Midwife's Apprentice*, found hers, and in my next book, Lucy Whipple finds hers.

And my place is full of words, of settings real and pretend, of people I have never met but know as well as I know myself, of events that never happened but have changed me in the imagining. This is why I write.

I write for the child I was and the child I still am. Like countless other lucky adults, I have much in common with children. We daydream, wonder, exaggerate, ask "what if?"—and what we imagine sometimes is more true than what is. We like to play with squishy things —mud, clay, dough, words—and we make stuff out of them. We like kids, animals, rain puddles, and pizza, and dare to love silly things. We don't like Brussels sprouts, the dentist, or books with great long passages of description, flashbacks or dream sequences. We like happy endings—or at least, hope. And we love stories.

There is a Hasidic story (there is always a Hasidic story):

Some followers go to their rabbi.

"Rebbe," they ask, "what is heaven like?"

"In heaven," answers the rabbi, "they sit at a table with all sorts of delicacies and good things. The only problem is their arms do not bend."

"And what is hell like?"

"In hell they sit at a table with all sorts of delicacies and good things. The only problem is their arms do not bend."

"Then, Rebbe, what is the difference between heaven and hell?"

"Ah, my children," said the rabbi, "in Heaven they feed each other."

Writing for me is us feeding each other— writer and reader—fifty-four-year-old me and the young people who pick up my books. Me whispering in their ears and them talking back. They read and I am nourished, and my book becomes something richer and more profound than I ever hoped.

After *Catherine, Called Birdy* was named a Newbery Honor Book last year, a number of interviewers remarked that I had come out of nowhere. I didn't. I always knew where I was. I just hadn't started whispering to the rice yet.[1]

As for what subjects to write about and which audience to write for, in numerous interviews, Cushman has discussed the important role her daughter and her daughter's friends have played in her choice to write fiction for adolescents. Obviously, her daughter didn't live in the Middle Ages; Cushman's inspiration to tackle historical fiction came from elsewhere. Before she wrote her first novel, Cushman found herself at a Renaissance fair, a festival where people dress up in medieval costumes, listen to medieval music, and play medieval games. At the fair, Cushman began wondering what it was like for a young girl to resist her narrow options when she didn't have much of a choice. Cushman insists that she never liked history class in school, which in her experience was mostly about memorizing names and dates, but she's intrigued by what life was like in other time periods.

The questions that motivate Cushman to write come from everywhere. As she says, her curiosity comes from "looking and listening, reading and living, wondering and doubting and failing." In fact, "ideas pour out of [her] ears and clutter up the floor all around [her] desk." As she says, "I will never live long enough to write about each one."[2]

Sometimes, Life Isn't Pretty

Critics both applaud and criticize Cushman for her use of gritty detail and unflinching realism. In other words, for "hold[ing] the reader's nose up to the stench [bad small] of history,"[3] as one critic put it. In addition to the sometimes grueling descriptions of the unhygienic conditions of the gold rush and the Middle Ages, there's also a severity in Cushman's descriptions of her characters' struggles. In particular, they can be bitter.

Many young adult novels contain characters that, although faced with challenges, never let go of a certain amount of naiveté and wide-eyed optimism. Perhaps this is how many adults prefer to view children, as being eternally hopeful. However, Cushman's characters are realistic, and as such, they can become depressed and embittered by their circumstances.

For example, Rodzina is not naive or optimistic about the tragedies that have led her to the orphan train. She knows that due to the tragedies she has suffered in her life, she's sometimes mean to adults and mistrustful of strangers. There's some cursing in Cushman's books, which some critics don't like, and even some physical abuse. A few critics have said that Cushman's female protagonists are not realistic with regard to fitting in with their respective time periods and settings. They say this because they are all so intelligent, strong-willed, independent-minded, and highly educated.

Cushman admits that placing such bright and willful girls in a medieval setting might be a stretch. Nonetheless, she contends that long ago, some of those young women must have wanted more out of life than what their circumstances offered. What about those who wanted better lives? Cushman's novels ask. How did they survive the frustration and disappointment of desiring more than they could have, and what became of them?

Cushman has said in interviews that accuracy—including grittiness—is essential to writing authentic historical fiction. What's the point of learning about a place and time if we change everything to fit our modern scope of what is acceptable? This is called relativism—just because we have certain modes of behavior and beliefs doesn't mean they are shared by people living in different times and places. For example, in other countries, people celebrate different holidays, worship different deities, or gods, and perform different rituals from those that are practiced in typical Anglo-Saxon cultures in the United States and Canada. In the Middle Ages, for example, beer was an acceptable drink for young people, and Cushman's characters drink it regularly, mostly because there wasn't much fresh, clean water.

Relating to the Past

Cushman is not concerned with making sure that her characters experience exactly what modern adolescents might experience. However, her intent is to create a sense of empathy, or understanding, that she hopes her readers will feel from reading her work. As she states, she wants to evoke a feeling of understanding that might be shared by young people living in different eras. She further explains this goal in her writing when she says, "Two people can be alike without living in the same place or era."[4]

Ultimately, as one reads Cushman's novels, it is inevitable that comparisons will be drawn between her main characters' lives and those of the readers'. In fact, this might not even be a tangible result of reading a Cushman novel. However, what Cushman wants is that her readers ask themselves questions such as: What would be the thing I would like least about being an adolescent in the Middle Ages? What would I like best? When have I had to grow accustomed to difficult circumstances? No matter which era Cushman's characters live in, each of them finds herself at odds with her surroundings and ultimately has to learn how to accept reality and make the best of it. Certainly this is something modern-day young adults also experience.

The Hard Part

How does Cushman turn her interest and ideas into books? The writing, Cushman admits, is the truly difficult part. There is almost always something more fun to do than sit down at a desk and stare at a computer screen. There are times when even laundry and dishes can be more appealing than writing. Like many authors, Cushman makes a point of writing every single day, and she reads just as often. She says that writers must always exercise their writing muscles in the same way that an athlete might train in order to achieve the best time in his or her event. Cushman studies the craft like any scholar studies his or her subject, though she admits that a large part of the process of writing is intuitive. She reads the work of other young adult authors because she loves the genre and likes to see how other people work, specifically Sharon Creech, Patricia MacLachlan, and Cynthia Rylant. As for studying her craft, Cushman has a natural writing talent and never pursued a formal education in writing, though of course many other successful authors do. Instead she learns as she goes, from reading others, and by writing draft after draft.

The Writing Process

For those who ever get the urge to write a story (or even a book), it's necessary to have as much privacy and space as possible. Professional writers know that their words don't always come easily, and the act of writing is anything but glamorous. Sometimes it's necessary to think and think for hours before even writing a single phrase. And after that sentence comes another, and another, and so on.

To help in the writing process, many writers give themselves goals to reach. For example, an author might insist on writing 1,000 words (about four typed pages) every day. Many writers also insist on having a clear, uncluttered, unshared, and comfortable workspace. This helps them give the act of writing a certain priority in their lives. Meanwhile, other writers set aside a particular time of the day to write, and during that time nothing else can interfere. No ringing phone, no doorbell, no chores, no surfing the Internet, and no washing the dishes. Just writing. Sitting and writing. Sitting. Writing. Until the story is finished.

Cushman claims that her favorite of her five novels is *The Midwife's Apprentice* because it came so easily to her. This was a marked contrast to *Catherine, Called Birdy*, which took her three years to research and write. In fact, when Cushman visits schools or other groups to talk about the writing process, she often brings with her the twenty-seven versions of *Catherine* that she wrote in order to show how grueling the process of writing and revising can be.

One thing is certain, though: the process might be grueling, but the experience of reading one of her novels is far from it. In fact, the whole thing seems almost weightless. Cushman's novels effortlessly carry the reader from page to page. The main characters she created are unfailingly charming even when they are behaving badly, which, like most adolescents, they often do. Cushman's readers and fans hope that she continues to do what she does best and that there will be many more examples of her dedication and hard work on bookstore shelves throughout the coming years.

Interview with Karen Cushman

This interview with Karen Cushman was published in "Author Spotlight: Karen Cushman," by Stephanie Loer, Education Place, © Houghton-Mifflin. The original interview can be found at http://www.eduplace.com/author/cushman/interview.html.

STEPHANIE LOER: Where do you get the ideas for your books?

KAREN CUSHMAN: My ideas come from reading and listening and living; they come from making mistakes and figuring things out. Ideas come from wondering a lot—such as what would happen if a certain situation occurred—and then, what would happen next?

STEPHANIE LOER: What do you find so inter-esting about the medieval times?

KAREN CUSHMAN: The time period appeals to me because I think of the Middle Ages moving into the Renaissance as like a child growing into ado-lescence. At this point in history, people began to have concerns about identity and concerns about appearance. Men and women began to pay atten-tion to how they looked, and all of a sudden, there were books written about manners. There were also concerns about accountability and privacy. These are some of the same issues that today's adolescents face.

STEPHANIE LOER: Are the feast days, noted with each journal entry in *Catherine, Called Birdy* authentic?

KAREN CUSHMAN: Yes, the feast days honoring saints are authentic. In fact, I just read a quote that said "by the year 1200, there were more than 25,000 saints." It was easy to become a saint in those days, because making a person a saint wasn't an official act of the Church.

I found most of my information about saints and what deeds were attributed to them in the

Oxford Dictionary of Saints. These were saints of England, because that's where the stories take place.

STEPHANIE LOER: Catherine uses the phrase "corpus bones" in many of her diary entries. What does it mean?

KAREN CUSHMAN: It apparently refers to the body of Christ. Or, if it's a corruption of the Latin word for good, it might mean "good body." Children ask about this particular phrase whenever I speak in a classroom, so I use it to make a point.

I did not document my source for "corpus bones." And I always point out that this is a very good lesson about the importance of documenting your research. I read the phrase, copied it into my notebook of language used during the Middle Ages, and did not record the source. I should have documented where I found it.

STEPHANIE LOER: What type of sources do you use for your novels?

KAREN CUSHMAN: I use general histories of the period and I search out as many primary sources as I can find. Primary sources are firsthand accounts of life and incidents in letter form, private journals, and personal papers. Then I read books about the manners, clothing, agriculture, foods, and even recipes of the period.

Readers will note that I list some of the sources in an author's note at the back of the books. Anyone who is interested in a subject can do research. All you need to do is find one good reference book and look up the bibliography. Select the books that interest you and start reading, recording and documenting.

STEPHANIE LOER: Why did you write *Catherine, Called Birdy* as a diary?

KAREN CUSHMAN: There were two reasons: I thought the diary form would give readers a more personal picture of this young girl in a time and place that may be very foreign to today's children. The diary form made the story more intimate and immediate.

The other reason was that diary entries allowed readers to see Catherine through their eyes and through her eyes at the same time. And the difference between the two points of view brought out a lot of humor, because Catherine, at times, took herself much more seriously than we would.

STEPHANIE LOER: What advice do you have for young people who would like to be authors?

KAREN CUSHMAN: Think of an idea or topic that is so strong within you that it's going to come out passionately as you write about it. Because that's what shines in a book. And then, do a lot of work—reading and research—to add layers of story to your idea.

STEPHANIE LOER: Your characters are very strong and memorable and I hate to say goodbye to them when I close the book. Do you ever plan to revisit any of them in future books?

KAREN CUSHMAN: I considered writing sequels, but I've realized that sequels often disappoint too many people. Different people have their own expectations for what should happen to characters, and the ideas are so varied that it would be difficult to write a sequel that would please everybody.

STEPHANIE LOER: A teacher states: *"Catherine, Called Birdy* and *The Midwife's Apprentice* are intriguing books. But I am quite uncomfortable about using crude language when such controversial elements fuel the fire for public censorship." Was it necessary to use such graphic descriptions and vulgar language?

KAREN CUSHMAN: I used those words because they are the words that were in general use at the time. They were not considered crude at the time. We think of them as crude today, but they were the generally accepted terms describing bodily functions in medieval times. I wanted the books to be as authentic as possible. And I think that is why people like the books, because the details ring true. It would be out of character to have the protagonists use words from another time.

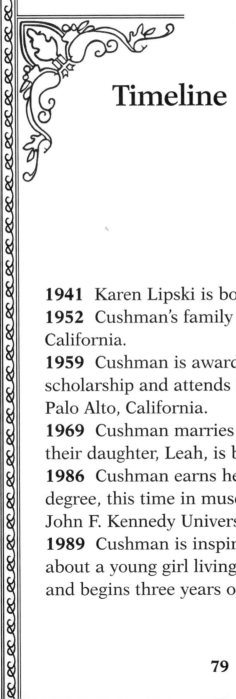

Timeline

1941 Karen Lipski is born in Chicago, Illinois.
1952 Cushman's family moves to Tarzana, California.
1959 Cushman is awarded a prestigious scholarship and attends Stanford University in Palo Alto, California.
1969 Cushman marries Philip Cushman, and their daughter, Leah, is born shortly after.
1986 Cushman earns her second master's degree, this time in museum studies, from John F. Kennedy University.
1989 Cushman is inspired to write a story about a young girl living in the Middle Ages and begins three years of research.

1994 *Catherine, Called Birdy* is published to rave reviews and is named a Newbery Honor Book. **1996** *The Midwife's Apprentice* wins the Newbery Medal.

Selected Reviews from *School Library Journal*

The Ballad of Lucy Whipple
1996

Gr 5–8—Following the death of Lucy's father, her mother moves her family from Massachusetts to the gold fields of California. Their home is now the rough-and-tumble gold-mining town of Lucky Diggins. Lucy feels distinctly out of place and longs for her grandparents and home. She tells of traveling west and settling down in this lonesome place, occasionally relating incidents through letters to her grandparents. She is a dreamy, bookish girl, not interested in the harsh life of the gold camps and California wilderness. Still, she makes unusual friends and has some adventures. Her brother, Butte, eleven, dies; her mother works hard in a boarding house for miners and falls in love with a traveling evangelist. Lucy matures considerably over the course of the book, in the end choosing to remain in California rather than return to Massachusetts or follow her sisters, mother, and her mother's new husband to the Sandwich Islands. Cushman's heroine is a delightful character, and the historical setting is authentically portrayed. Lucy's story, as the author points out in her end notes, is the story of many pioneer women who exhibited great strength and courage as they helped to settle the West. The book is full of small details that children will love. Butte, for example, collects almost fifty words for liquor; listing them takes up half of a page. Young readers will enjoy this story, and it will make a great tie-in to American history lessons.

Catherine, Called Birdy
1994

Gr 6–9—The fourteen-year-old daughter of a rustic knight records the events of her days in the year 1290, writing perceptive, scathing, and often raucously funny observations about her family, friends, and would-be suitors. A delightful, rebellious heroine, determined not to marry the man of her father's choice.

Matilda Bone
2000

Gr 4–8—A fascinating glimpse into the colorful life and times of the fourteenth century. Orphaned Matilda, thirteen, has lived the good life in a manor where she was well educated by Father Leufredus. Things change drastically, however, when he abandons her, leaving her to serve as an assistant to a bonesetter in return for food and shelter. Matilda is expected to cook the meals, tend the fire, and generally assist Red Peg. And Peg has her hands full dealing with this self-righteous, pious child who snobbishly sprinkles Latin in her everyday speech and continuously brags about her ability to read and write. Peg, however, allows Matilda time to ponder her new role and teaches her, by example, that kindness and friendship go a long way toward lessening the harshness of life in this small English village. Matilda constantly prays for help, guidance, and deliverance. The saints, and this child knows many, respond with humor and sometimes sound advice. The theology espoused by Matilda is consistent with the time period and Father Leufredus has taught her well. She has no thoughts of her own—only the musings and learning of Father Leufredus. She stiffly withholds herself from all attempts at friendship and kindness, and she feels more and more alone. However, when she meets a kitchen maid who joyfully introduces her to the market square, her eyes slowly open to the world around her. Readers witness her spiritual and emotional growth as she blossoms from a self-centered "nincompoop" to a compassionate, competent assistant. Cushman's character descriptions are spare, with each word carefully chosen to paint wonderful pictures. This humorous, frank look at life in the medical quarters in medieval times shows readers that love and compassion, laughter and companionship, are indeed the best medicine.

The Midwife's Apprentice
1995

Gr 6–9—With simplicity, wit, and humor, Cushman presents another tale of medieval England. Here, readers follow the satisfying, literal, and figurative journey of a homeless, nameless child called Brat, who might be twelve or thirteen—no one really knows. She wandered about in her early years, seeking food and any kind of refuge and, like many outsiders, gained a certain kind of wisdom about people and their ways. Still, life held little purpose beyond survival until she meets the sharp-nosed, irritable local midwife, which is where this story begins. Jane takes her in, re-names her Beetle, and thinks of her as free labor and no competition. Always practical but initially timid, the girl expands in courage and self-awareness, acquiring a cat as a companion, naming herself Alyce, and gaining experience in the ways of midwifery. From the breathless delight of helping a boy to deliver twin calves, to the despair of failure during a difficult birth, to the triumph of a successful delivery, Alyce struggles to understand how she can allow herself to fail and yet have the determination to reach for her own place in the world. Alyce wins. Characters are sketched briefly but with telling, witty detail, and the very scents and sounds of the land and people's occupations fill each page as Alyce comes of age and heart. Earthy humor, the foibles of humans both high and low, and a fascinating mix of superstition and genuinely helpful herbal remedies attached to childbirth make this a truly delightful introduction to a world seldom seen in children's literature.

Rodzina
2003

Gr 4–7—It is 1881, and twelve-year-old Rodzina Clara Jadwiga Anastazya Brodski finds herself on an orphan train bound from Chicago to the west where, she is sure, she will be sold into slavery. All of her family members have died tragically, and the large, unpretty, and standoffish girl can't believe she will be adopted into a loving home. Pressed into service to help with the younger children by tough Mr. Szprot and a stern young woman whom she calls Miss Doctor, Rodzina entertains the youngsters with colorful stories from her Polish heritage and watches as the more appealing children are adopted along the way. She, too, is placed twice, with a pair of nasty old sisters in need of a servant and once with a crude farmer looking for a wife to replace the dying mother of his thirteen children, but each time she escapes and returns to the train. As the journey progresses, she repeatedly reaches out to the woman doctor who, caught up in her own plight to be accepted in her profession, continually rebuffs the girl until the dual crisis of a lost child and Rodzina's own attempt to run away finally begin to break down the barrier between them. The story features engaging characters, a vivid setting, and a prickly but endearing heroine. The first-person narrative captures the personality and spirit of a child grieving for her lost family, yet resourceful and determined to make her own way. Rodzina's musings and observations provide poignancy, humor, and a keen sense of the human and topographical landscape.

Selected reviews from *School Library Journal* reproduced with permission from *School Library Journal,* copyright © 1994, 1995, 1996, 2000, 2003 by Cahners Business Information, a division of Reed Elsevier, Inc.

List of Selected Works

The Ballad of Lucy Whipple. New York, NY: Clarion, 1996.

Catherine, Called Birdy. New York, NY: Clarion, 1994.

Matilda Bone. New York, NY: Clarion, 2001.

The Midwife's Apprentice. New York, NY: Clarion, 1995.

Rodzina. New York, NY: Clarion, 2003.

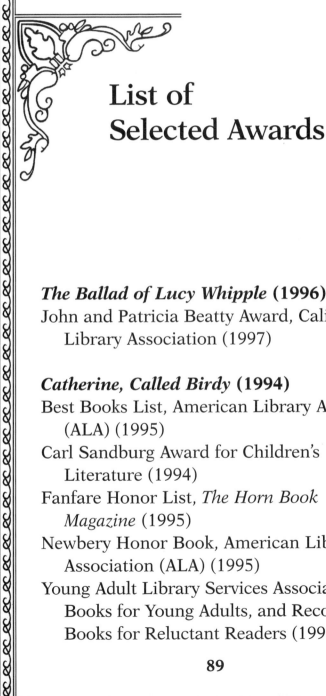

List of
Selected Awards

***The Ballad of Lucy Whipple* (1996)**
John and Patricia Beatty Award, California
   Library Association (1997)

***Catherine, Called Birdy* (1994)**
Best Books List, American Library Association
   (ALA) (1995)
Carl Sandburg Award for Children's
   Literature (1994)
Fanfare Honor List, *The Horn Book*
   Magazine (1995)
Newbery Honor Book, American Library
   Association (ALA) (1995)
Young Adult Library Services Association Best
   Books for Young Adults, and Recommended
   Books for Reluctant Readers (1995)

The Midwife's Apprentice (1995)

Booklist Editors' Choice, American Library Association (ALA) (1996)

Newbery Medal, American Library Association (ALA) (1996)

Pick of the Lists, American Bookseller Association (1995)

Recommended Book, New York Public Library (1995)

Young Adult Library Services Association Best Books for Young Adults (1995)

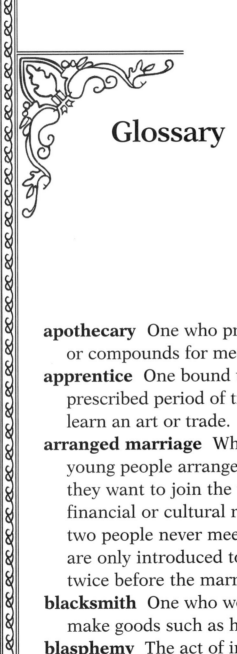

Glossary

apothecary One who prepares and sells drugs or compounds for medicinal purposes.

apprentice One bound to serve another for a prescribed period of time. The goal is to learn an art or trade.

arranged marriage When the parents of two young people arrange a marriage because they want to join the two families for financial or cultural reasons. Often, the two people never meet. Oftentimes, they are only introduced to each other once or twice before the marriage ceremony.

blacksmith One who works with iron to make goods such as horseshoes.

blasphemy The act of insulting or showing contempt or lack of reverence for God.

Brace, Charles Loring Founder of the Children's Aid Society, which started the orphan train to help place orphans in New York City with parents across the country.

Crusades Military expeditions during the eleventh to thirteenth centuries in which Christians waged war against non-Christians, specifically Muslims, in order to keep other religions from spreading in Europe.

dismay Disappointment.

doctorate The degree, title, or rank of a doctor.

empathy The action of understanding, being aware of, and being sensitive to another's feelings.

feast days Celebrations that were typical in the Middle Ages. Feast days were meant to honor the lives of saints.

genre A category of artistic, musical, or literary composition characterized by a particular style, form, or content.

gnome According to folklore, an ageless and often deformed dwarf who lives in the earth and usually guards treasure.

hierarchy The classification of a group of people according to ability or economic, social, or professional status.

historical fiction A fictional story set in a true historical setting.

horticultural Having to do with plants.

humors In medieval physiology, one of the four fluids entering into the constitution of the body and determining by their relative proportions a person's health and temperament.

incantation The use of spells or verbal charms spoken or sung as a part of a ritual of magic.

inquisitive Curious.

intuitive Insightful and very aware of one's surroundings—including people.

manor A large house in the Middle Ages consisting of an estate under a lord enjoying a variety of rights over its land and tenants.

metropolis A thriving city, densely populated and urban.

midwife A person who assists women in childbirth.

miners People who look for metals, including gold, by digging in the earth.

museum studies The study of how to interpret artifacts, maintain collections of artifacts and art, and design museum exhibits.

noble One who is of high birth or exalted rank.

orphan train A program developed in 1853 by the New York Children's Aid Society to provide thousands of street children with homes in rural communities in the American Midwest.

pageantry A colorful, rich, or splendid display.

persecution The act of harassing in a manner designed to injure or cause suffering, usually based on race, religion, or other points of discrimination.

physiology The science of the functions and activities of life or of living matter.

plot-driven A story in which the specifics of the plot direct the actions of a character.

primary source Firsthand account, such as a letter or diary.

prism A medium that distorts, slants, or colors whatever is viewed through it.

privy An outdoor toilet, similar to an outhouse.

protagonist The main character in a novel.

rabbinical Relating to rabbis or their writings.

relativism The view that ethics and behavior differ depending on with whom and when they occur.

relic A trace of some past or outmoded practice, custom, or belief. A relic can also be an actual object that dates from a specific time.

Renaissance The transitional movement in Europe between medieval and modern times that began in the fourteenth century in Italy. This lasted into the seventeenth century and was marked by an intense revival of the arts and literature, as well as the beginnings of modern science.

rural In the country or an agricultural area.

saint One officially recognized as exceptionally holy by the Catholic Church.

secondary source Source that is written at a time much later than the period it describes.

suitor An old-fashioned term describing someone who courts a girl or woman in an effort to marry her.

theme The underlying message or moral, usually repeated throughout a novel.

virtuous Very moral.

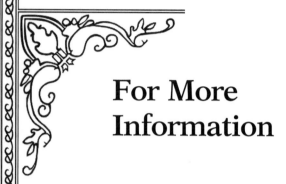

For More Information

Web Sites

Due to the changing nature of Internet links, the Rosen Publishing Group, Inc., has developed an online list of Web sites related to the subject of this book. This site is updated regularly. Please use this link to access the list:

http://www.rosenlinks.com/lab/kacu

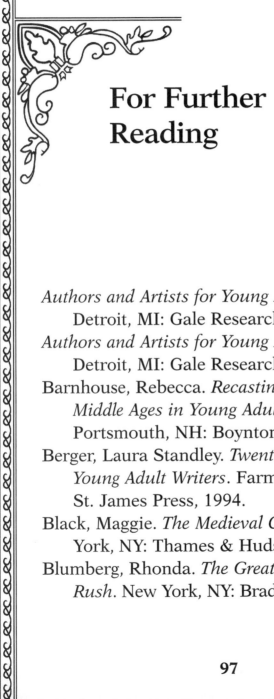

For Further Reading

Authors and Artists for Young Adults. Vol. 1. Detroit, MI: Gale Research, 1989.

Authors and Artists for Young Adults. Vol. 31. Detroit, MI: Gale Research, 1989.

Barnhouse, Rebecca. *Recasting the Past: The Middle Ages in Young Adult Literature.* Portsmouth, NH: Boynton/Cook, 2000.

Berger, Laura Standley. *Twentieth-Century Young Adult Writers.* Farmington Hills, MI: St. James Press, 1994.

Black, Maggie. *The Medieval Cookbook.* New York, NY: Thames & Hudson, 1996.

Blumberg, Rhonda. *The Great American Gold Rush.* New York, NY: Bradbury Press, 1989.

Children's Literature Review. Vol. 3. Detroit, MI: The Gale Group, 2003.

Children's Literature Review. Vol. 55. Detroit, MI: The Gale Group, 2000.

Corbishley, Mike. *The Middle Ages.* New York, NY: Checkmark Books, 1990.

Farmer, David. *The Oxford Dictionary of Saints.* Fifth edition. Oxford, England: Oxford University Press, 2003.

Fry, Annette. *The Orphan Trains.* New York, NY: New Discovery Books, 1994.

Gallo, Donald R., ed. *Speaking for Ourselves, Too: More Autobiographical Sketches by Notable Authors of Books for Young Adults.* Urbana, IL: National Council of Teachers of English, 1993.

Hanawalt, Barbara A. *The Middle Ages: An Illustrated History.* Oxford, England: Oxford University Press, 1998.

Hedblad, Alan, ed. *Something About the Author.* Vol. 147. Detroit, MI: The Gale Group, 2000.

MacDonald, Fiona. *How Would You Survive in the Middle Ages?* New York, NY: Franklin Watts, 1997.

Nakamura, Joyce, ed. *Something About the Author, Autobiography Series.* Vol. 13. Detroit, MI: Gale Research, 1992.

Orphan Train Heritage Society of America (OTHSA). *Orphan Train Riders: Their Own*

Stories. Vols. 1–4. Baltimore, MD: Gateway Press, Inc., 1992, 1993.

Twentieth Century Young Adult Writers. Farmington Hills, MI: St. James Press, 1994.

Warren, Andrea. *All Aboard the Orphan Trains*. New York, NY: Ticknor & Fields, 1995.

Warren, Andrea. *Orphan Train Rider: One Boy's True Story*. Boston, MA: Houghton Mifflin, 1995.

Warren, Andrea. *We Rode the Orphan Trains*. Boston, MA: Houghton Mifflin, 2001.

Bibliography

Aronson, Marc. "When Coming of Age Meets the Age That's Coming." *Voice of Youth Advocates*, Vol. 21, No. 4, October 1998, pp. 261–263.

Bostrom, Kathleen Long. *Winning Authors: Profiles of the Newbery Medalists*. Westport, CT: Libraries Unlimited, 2003.

California Department of Parks & Recreation. "Gold Rush Overview." Retrieved February 2005 (http://www.ca.gov/s/history/cahdream.html).

California Gold Rush Band, official site. "Music of the California Gold Rush Band." Retrieved February 2005 (http://expage.com/page/cgrbmusic).

Cushman, Karen. "Acceptance Speech."
    Houghton Mifflin Education Place. Retrieved
    November 2004 (http://www.eduplace.com/
    author/cushman/speech.html).

Cushman, Karen. *The Ballad of Lucy Whipple*.
    New York, NY: Clarion Books, 1996.

Cushman, Karen. *Catherine, Called Birdy*. New
    York, NY: Clarion Books, 1994.

Cushman, Karen. *Matilda Bone*. New York, NY:
    Clarion Books, 2001.

Cushman, Karen. *The Midwife's Apprentice*. New
    York, NY: Clarion Books, 1995.

Cushman, Karen. *Rodzina*. New York, NY:
    Clarion Books, 2003.

Drew, Bernard. *100 More Popular Young Adult
    Authors*. Westport, CT: Libraries
    Unlimited, 2002.

Edwards, Eden K. Essay in *Children's Books and
    Their Creators*, edited by Anita Silvey. Boston,
    MA: Houghton Mifflin, 1995.

Gallo, Don. "What Should Teachers Know
    About YA Lit for 2004?" *English Journal*,
    November 1984.

Gallo, Donald R., ed. *Speaking for Ourselves:
    Autobiographical Sketches by Notable Authors
    of Books for Young Adults*. Urbana, IL:
    National Council of Teachers of English, 1990.

Gode Cookery. "Tales of the Middle Ages:
Daily Life." Retrieved February 2005
(http://www. godecookery.com/mtales/
mtales08.htm).

Goldrush World Access. "The Women." Retrieved
February 2005 (http://www.goldrush.com/
~joann/women.htm).

HarperCollins. *A Guide to Teaching*. Retrieved
May 2004 (http://www.harperchildrens.com/
schoolhouse/TeachersGuides/
cushmanindex.htm).

Hedblad, Alan, ed. *Something About the Author*.
Vol. 147. Detroit, MI: The Gale Group, 2000.

Holmes Holtze, Sally, ed. *Sixth Book of Junior
Authors and Illustrators*. New York, NY:
H. W. Wilson Co., 1989.

Internet Public Library. "Karen Cushman."
Retrieved May 2004 (http://www.ipl.org/div/
kidspace/askauthor/cushmanbio.html).

Jackson, Richard. "We." *Horn Book Magazine*,
May/June 1993.

Johnson, Mary Ellen. OrphanTrainRiders.com.
"A History of the Orphan Trains Era in
American History." Retrieved July 2004
(http://www.orphantrainriders.com).

Kyerene de las Brisas Elementary. "Life in the
Middle Ages." Retrieved February 2005

(http://www.kyrene.k12.az.us/schools/Brisas/
sunda/ma/mahome.htm).

Madrigal, Alix. "What If Your Mom Dragged You
to the Gold Rush?" *San Francisco Chronicle*,
September 29, 1996.

Malakoff & Co. "James W. Marshall's Account of
the First Discovery of Gold." Retrieved
February 2005 (http://www.malakoff.com/
marshall.htm).

Merryman, Kathleen. "Stubborn Girls Who Find
a Way." *The News Tribune* (Tacoma, WA),
February 11, 1998.

Mitchell, Sean. "Grown-up Author's Insights into
Adolescent Struggles." *Dallas Times Herald*,
June 27, 1979.

O'Reilly, Jane. "On the Orphan Train." *New York
Times Book Review*, May 18, 2003.

PBSKids.org. "Gold Rush for Teachers and
Parents." Retrieved February 2005
(http://pbskids.org/wayback/goldrush/tp.html).

PBS Online—The American Experience. "The
Orphan Trains." The WGBH Educational
Foundation. Retrieved July 2004
(http://www.pbs.org/wgbh/amex/orphan).

Pendergast, Tom, and Sara Pendergast, eds. *St.
James Guide to Young Adult Writers*. 2nd
edition. Detroit, MI: St. James Press, 1999.

Seventh Book of Junior Authors and Illustrators. New York, NY: H. W. Wilson Co., 1996.

Spencer, Pam. *What Do Young Adults Read Next? A Reader's Guide to Fiction for Young Adults.* Detroit, MI: Gale Research, 1994.

Twentieth Century Young Adult Writers. Farmington Hills, MI: St. James Press, 1994.

Source Notes

Introduction

1. Alan Hedblad, ed. *Something About the Author*, Vol. 147 (Detroit, MI: Gale Group, 2000).
2. Karen Cushman interview with Internet Public Library. The regents of the University of Michigan. Retrieved May 2004 (http://www.ipl.org/div/kidspace/askauthor/cushmanbio.html).
3. Alan Hedblad, ed. *Something About the Author*, Vol. 147 (Detroit, MI: Gale Group, 2000).
4. Karen Cushman. "Acceptance Speech." Education Place Author Spotlight. Retrieved November 2004 (http://www.eduplace.com/author/cushman/speech.html).

Chapter 1

1. Karen Cushman. "Acceptance Speech." Education Place Author Spotlight. Retrieved

November 2004 (http://www.eduplace.com/
author/cushman/speech.html).

2. Karen Cushman. *Catherine, Called Birdy* (New
York, NY: Clarion Books, 1994), p. 69.

3. Alan Hedblad, ed. *Something About the Author*,
Vol. 147 (Detroit, MI: Gale Group, 2000).

4. *Twentieth Century Young Adult Writers* (Farmington
Hills, MI: St. James Press, 1994), p. 31.

5. Karen Cushman. "Acceptance Speech." Education
Place Author Spotlight. Retrieved November 2004
(http://www.eduplace.com/author/cushman/
speech.html).

6. Kathleen Merryman. "Stubborn Girls Who Find a
Way." *The News Tribune* (Tacoma, Washington),
February 11, 1998.

7. Karen Cushman. *Catherine, Called Birdy* (New
York, NY: Clarion Books, 1994), dedication.

8. Karen Cushman. "Acceptance Speech." Education
Place Author Spotlight. Retrieved November 2004
(http://www.eduplace.com/author/cushman/
speech.html).

9. Alan Hedblad, ed. *Something About the Author*,
Vol. 147 (Detroit, MI: Gale Group, 2000).

10. Alix Madrigal. "What If Your Mom Dragged You
to the Gold Rush?" *San Francisco Chronicle*,
September 29, 1996, p. 10.

Chapter 2

1. Alan Hedblad, ed. *Something About the Author*,
Vol. 147 (Detroit, MI: Gale Group, 2000).

2. Karen Cushman. *Matilda Bone* (New York, NY: Clarion Books, 2001), p. 161.
3. Karen Cushman. *The Ballad of Lucy Whipple* (New York, NY: Clarion Books, 1996), p. 32.

Chapter 3

1. Karen Cushman. *Catherine, Called Birdy* (New York, NY: Clarion Books, 1994), pp. 4–5.
2. Kathleen Merryman. "Stubborn Girls Who Find a Way." *The News Tribune* (Tacoma, Washington), February 11, 1998, p. 1.
3. Karen Cushman interview with Internet Public Library. The regents of the University of Michigan. Retrieved May 2004 (http://www.ipl.org/div/kidspace/askauthor/cushmanbio.html).
4. Karen Cushman interview with AuthorChats. Retrieved November 2004 (http://www.authorchats.com).
5. Karen Cushman. *Catherine, Called Birdy* (New York, NY: Clarion Books, 1994), p. 8.
6. Karen Cushman. *Matilda Bone* (New York, NY: Clarion Books, 2001), p. 5.
7. Karen Cushman. *Catherine, Called Birdy* (New York, NY: Clarion Books, 1994), p. 118.
8. HarperCollins. "A Guide to Teaching." Retrieved May 2004 (http://www.harperchildrens.com/schoolhouse/TeachersGuides/cushmanindex.htm).

Chapter 4

1. Karen Cushman. "Acceptance Speech." Education Place Author Spotlight. Retrieved November 2004

(http://www.eduplace.com/author/cushman/speech.html).

2. HarperCollins. "A Guide to Teaching." Retrieved May 2004 (http://www.harperchildrens.com/schoolhouse/TeachersGuides/cushmanindex.htm).

3. Alan Hedblad, ed. *Something About the Author*, Vol. 147 (Detroit, MI: Gale Group, 2000).

4. *Twentieth Century Young Adult Writers* (Farmington Hills, MI: St. James Press, 1994), p. 32.

Index

About the Author

Susanna Daniel is a writer and editor, and an adjunct instructor of creative writing and composition at Madison Area Technical College, in Madison, Wisconsin. Her fiction has been published in *Best New American Voices 2001*, as well as *Epoch Magazine* and the *Madison Review*. She is at work on a novel set in her hometown of Miami, Florida.

Photo Credits

Cover © Crescent Studios, Vashon, WA, courtesy of Houghton Mifflin; p. 2 © Fred Mertz, courtesy of HarperCollins.

Series Designer: Tahara Anderson
Photo Researcher: Hillary Arnold